Dachshunds

Dachshunds Owner's Care Guide

Dachshund Breeding, Diet, Adoption, Temperament, Where to Buy, Cost, Health, Lifespan, Types, and Much More Included!

By: Lolly Brown

Foreword

The Dachshund may very well be one of the most distinguishable dog breeds, easy to recognize for its long body and short, stubby legs. This breed may be a little strange in appearance but the Dachshund has a number of qualities which make it a great breed. Not only are Dachshunds talented hunters for small prey, but they also excel in field trials and other dog sports. Despite the small size and odd looks of this breed, it has many redeeming qualities that make it truly unique.

If you are considering getting a Dachshund as a pet, you would be wise to learn as much as you can about these dogs before you make your decision. Dachshunds are small in size and playful by nature but they can be a little bit stubborn at times and may be difficult to train. Taking the time to familiarize yourself with the breed will help you to decide whether or not it is really the best option for you. If it is, you will find all of the information you need in this book to introduce you to the Dachshund breed and to get you started on your way to becoming the best Dachshund owner that you can possibly be.

Table of Contents

Introduction

The chances are good that when you hear the word "Dachshund" you picture a small dog with short, stubby legs and a long body. There is no denying the fact that Dachshunds are an easy breed to identify, but there is so much more to learn about them than their unique appearance and small size. These little dogs are smart and trainable, plus they love to spend time with family – they make great family pets with proper training.

If you are thinking about getting a Dachshund as a pet, take the time to learn everything you can about this wonderful breed. Many dog breeds have similar basic requirements for care and nutrition but, if you really want your Dachshund to thrive, you need to know the specifics about his care requirements. Luckily, that is exactly what this book will teach you!

Within the pages of this book you will find a wealth of information about the Dachshund breed. Here you will learn about the breed's history and receive some helpful Dachshund facts about their appearance, temperament, and personality. By the time you finish this book you should not only have a deeper understanding of the Dachshund breed but you will also know whether it is the right breed for you. If it is, you will be well on your way to becoming the best Dachshund owner you can possibly be!

So, if you are ready to learn more about the Dachshund breed simply turn the page and keep reading!

Glossary of Dog Terms

AKC – American Kennel Club, the largest purebred dog registry in the United States

Almond Eye – Referring to an elongated eye shape rather than a rounded shape

Apple Head – A round-shaped skull

Balance – A show term referring to all of the parts of the dog, both moving and standing, which produce a harmonious image

Beard – Long, thick hair on the dog's underjaw

Best in Show – An award given to the only undefeated dog left standing at the end of judging

Bitch – A female dog

Bite – The position of the upper and lower teeth when the dog's jaws are closed; positions include level, undershot, scissors, or overshot

Blaze – A white stripe running down the center of the face between the eyes

Board – To house, feed, and care for a dog for a fee

Breed – A domestic race of dogs having a common gene pool and characterized appearance/function

Breed Standard – A published document describing the look, movement, and behavior of the perfect specimen of a particular breed

Buff – An off-white to gold coloring

Clip – A method of trimming the coat in some breeds

Coat – The hair covering of a dog; some breeds have two coats, and outer coat and undercoat; also known as a double coat. Examples of breeds with double coats include German Shepherd, Siberian Husky, Akita, etc.

Condition – The health of the dog as shown by its skin, coat, behavior, and general appearance

Crate – A container used to house and transport dogs; also called a cage or kennel

Crossbreed (Hybrid) – A dog having a sire and dam of two different breeds; cannot be registered with the AKC

Dam (bitch) – The female parent of a dog;

Dock – To shorten the tail of a dog by surgically removing the end part of the tail.

Double Coat – Having an outer weather-resistant coat and a soft, waterproof coat for warmth; see above.

Drop Ear – An ear in which the tip of the ear folds over and hangs down; not prick or erect

Entropion – A genetic disorder resulting in the upper or lower eyelid turning in

Fancier – A person who is especially interested in a particular breed or dog sport

Fawn – A red-yellow hue of brown

Feathering – A long fringe of hair on the ears, tail, legs, or body of a dog

Groom – To brush, trim, comb or otherwise make a dog's coat neat in appearance

Heel – To command a dog to stay close by its owner's side

Hip Dysplasia – A condition characterized by the abnormal formation of the hip joint

Inbreeding – The breeding of two closely related dogs of one breed

Kennel – A building or enclosure where dogs are kept

Litter – A group of puppies born at one time

Markings – A contrasting color or pattern on a dog's coat

Mask – Dark shading on the dog's foreface

Mate – To breed a dog and a bitch

Neuter – To castrate a male dog or spay a female dog

Pads – The tough, shock-absorbent skin on the bottom of a dog's foot

Parti-Color – A coloration of a dog's coat consisting of two or more definite, well-broken colors; one of the colors must be white

Pedigree – The written record of a dog's genealogy going back three generations or more

Pied – A coloration on a dog consisting of patches of white and another color

Prick Ear – Ear that is carried erect, usually pointed at the tip of the ear

Puppy – A dog under 12 months of age

Purebred – A dog whose sire and dam belong to the same breed and who are of unmixed descent

Saddle – Colored markings in the shape of a saddle over the back; colors may vary

Shedding – The natural process whereby old hair falls off the dog's body as it is replaced by new hair growth.

Sire – The male parent of a dog

Smooth Coat – Short hair that is close-lying

Spay – The surgery to remove a female dog's ovaries, rendering her incapable of breeding

Trim – To groom a dog's coat by plucking or clipping

Undercoat – The soft, short coat typically concealed by a longer outer coat

Wean – The process through which puppies transition from subsisting on their mother's milk to eating solid food

Whelping – The act of birthing a litter of puppies

Chapter One: Understanding Dachshunds

In this chapter you will find a wealth of basic information about the Dachshund breed including facts about Dachshunds, insight into their temperament, tips for training, and a brief history of the breed. The information in this chapter is intended to introduce you to the breed so you can start forming an idea about whether or not a Dachshund would be a good pet for you and your family. In the next chapter you will receive practical information about keeping Dachshund dogs to help you further in making this difficult but important decision.

Facts About Dachshund Dogs

Even if you have never seen or interacted with a Dachshund in person, you probably already know what they look like. Sometimes called "wiener dogs," Dachshunds are known for their long bodies and their short, stubby legs. Though they may not look like it, Dachshunds are actually talented hunting dogs – they were developed to scent and chase burrowing game like badgers, flushing them from their underground burrows so the hunter could shoot them. The miniature Dachshund breed was bred specifically for hunting small prey like rabbits.

Though they were originally developed for hunting, the Dachshund plays many roles today. In the U.S., the breed has been used to track wounded animals and they are also frequent participants in field trials, conformation shows, and other dog sports. According to American Kennel Club (AKC) registration statistics, the Dachshund is the 10th most popular breed in the United States. With dozens of different breeds accepted by the AKC, this is no small feat.

While all Dachshunds exhibit the characteristic long body and short legs, there are a number of breed differentiations in terms of size, coat and color. There are three different coat types seen in the Dachshund breed: smooth, longhaired, and wirehaired. The smooth coat variety is the shortest hair and it comes in an unlimited array of colors and patterns. The longhaired variety has a long, silky coat with ample feathering on the ears and legs. The wirehaired coat has a medium-length coat that is harsh and wiry in texture. This coat variety is the least common in the United States but it is very popular in various European countries, particularly in Germany.

In terms of color and pattern, Dachshunds vary greatly and there is no standard coloration. Many Dachshunds have a single base color of red or cream and many exhibit a pointed coloration of tan color points paired with another base color like black, brown, or blue. Tan color points appear as markings over the eyes, ears, paws, and tail. Other patterns that may occur in Dachshunds include merle, sable, piebald, and brindle. It is possible for a single litter of Dachshunds to exhibit a wide range of colors and patterns.

In addition to having long bodies, Dachshunds also have fairly long snouts. Their muzzles are long and somewhat tapered toward a dark nose and they have large, floppy ears that hang down on either side of their heads. The AKC prefers darker eye colors in Dachshunds, though a range from light brown or amber all the way to green is possible in this breed. It is also possible for Dachshunds to have two different colored eyes, though it is typically only seen in dapple pattern Dachshunds.

In terms of their size, Dachshunds do vary. There are three different sizes – standard, miniature, and kaninchen. The standard Dachshunds stands 8 to 9 inches tall and weighs 16 to 32 pounds at maturity while the miniature Dachshund stands 5 to 6 inches tall and weighs up to 11 pounds. The kaninchen variety is the smallest and its name comes from the German word for rabbit – this variety grows to a maximum size between 8 and 11 pounds.

When it comes to the temperament of the Dachshund breed, there is a great deal of variation. For the most part, Dachshunds are playful and lively companions – they form strong attachments with family and they can be protective in the presence of strangers. These dogs do have a tendency to bark and they can actually be very aggressive against strangers in some cases. According to a 2008 study conducted by the University of Pennsylvania, Dachshunds were rated by 6,000 dog owners as the most aggressive breed with 20% of them having bitten someone. Because these dogs are so small, the injuries caused by these attacks is not as severe as it would be with larger breeds but it is still important to consider.

With the aggressive tendencies of the breed being so clear, it is absolutely essential that you train and socialize your Dachshund from a very young age and maintain that kind of training throughout his life. Dachshunds are smart and generally very trainable, though they do have a tendency to develop a stubborn streak, as is common with small-breed dogs. Also common with smaller dogs, the Dachshund can be a little tricky to housebreak but most owners find that crate training methods are effective.

Aside from their potential to become aggressive with strangers, Dachshunds are generally loyal and affectionate with family. They are fairly active and do enjoy training for dog sports, though they really only need a moderate amount of exercise on a daily basis. Dachshunds may not be a good choice for children, though they can be okay when raised from a young age in the presence of children – the same is true for keeping Dachshunds with other dogs. In terms of their behavior around other pets, you should not be surprised if your Dachshund chases cats and other small animals due to their hunting background.

As a small-breed dog, the Dachshund has a very long lifespan averaging around 12 to 15 years. These dogs are unfortunately prone to a number of serious genetic health problems, particularly back problems. Intervertebral disk disease is common in Dachshunds, as are other musculoskeletal issues like patellar luxation. Many Dachshunds develop eye problems like progressive retinal atrophy, cataracts, or glaucoma and they are also prone to skin allergies and other skin conditions. It may surprise you to know that Dachshunds also have a high risk for gastric torsion, a condition more commonly seen in large and giant breeds – this is due to their deep-chested stature.

Summary of Dachshund Facts

Pedigree: origins may be traced to ancient Egypt; modern breed developed from European hounds and terriers

AKC Group: Hound Group

Breed Size: small

Height: 8 to 9 inches (Standard); 4 to 6 inches (Miniature)

Weight: 16 to 32 pounds (Standard); up to 11 pounds (Miniature); 8 to 11 pounds (Kaninchen)

Coat Length: smooth, longhaired or wirehaired

Coat Texture: soft and short; long and silky with feathering on the ears and legs; medium-length, harsh and wiry

Color: many colors and patterns; base color of red or cream is common, often with tan color points; no standard color

Eyes and Nose: ranges from amber to dark brown or green; AKC prefers darker colors

Ears: large, floppy drop ears

Tail: medium-length, thin and tapered

Temperament: playful, smart, active, clever, sometimes stubborn, prone to barking

Strangers: may bark at strangers, good watch dog

Children: may not be a good choice for young children

Other Dogs: generally good with other dogs if properly trained and socialized; may bark at other dogs

Training: intelligent and trainable but can develop a stubborn streak; may be tricky to housebreak

Exercise Needs: playful and active; need a moderate amount of exercise; prone to problem behaviors with boredom

Health Conditions: back problems, disc injuries, gastric torsion, diabetes, epilepsy, eye problems, skin conditions, obesity, patellar luxation

Lifespan: average 12 to 15 years

Dachshund Breed History

The exact origins of the Dachshund breed are unknown, though there is some evidence to suggest that early ancestors of the breed may go all the way back to ancient Egypt. Discoveries have been made of engravings of short-legged hunting dogs and there is a recent discovery that was made by the American University in Cairo of a mummified Dachshund-like dog found in ancient Egyptian burial urns. The modern version of the breed, however, is the product of selective breeding by German breeders.

The breed currently known as the Dachshund was developed by German breeders and it includes different hereditary elements drawn from various French, German, and English hounds and terriers. Originally bred for hunting badgers, the Dachshund breed has been kept in royal courts all over Europe – even by Queen Victoria. The first historical reference to the breed that has been verified comes from books written during the early 18th century – these texts mention "badger dogs" named "Dachs Kriecher" (badger crawler) and Dachs Krieger (badger warrior).

Early Dachshunds in Germany were much larger than the modern version of the breed – they typically weighed between 30 and 40 pounds. These dogs were used for scenting and hunting a variety of smaller game, though they were also used for tracking wounded deer and hunting game as large as wild boars in packs. There are multiple theories regarding the development of the longhaired and wirehaired varieties, though most involve crossing the Dachshund with various terrier breeds as well as small spaniels and other dogs.

The Dachshund breed first appeared in the United States in 1870 when it was imported as a rabbit hunting breed. The first Dachshund was registered by the American Kennel Club in 1885 and the first breed club in America (the Dachshund Club of America) was formed in 1895. The popularity of the breed declined drastically during World War I but it was built back up over the following decades to become one of the top 10 breeds in the country today.

Types of Dachshunds

There is only one Dachshund breed, but there are many variations in terms of size and coat length. As you have already learned, there are three different sizes for the Dachshund breed – standard, miniature, and kaninchen. You also know that there are three different coat types – smooth, longhaired, and wirehaired. To give you a better understanding of the differences between these types of Dachshunds you will find some useful information in the following pages:

Smooth Coated Dachshund

Dachshunds of this variety are the most common in the United States. These dogs have short, shiny coats that are smooth in texture and need very little grooming. Because their coats are so short, shedding may not be as noticeable as with other coat types, but it is still present. Also, because their coats are short, they may need an extra layer of protection against the cold in winter. For colorations, smooth coated Dachshunds are commonly seen in combinations of red, cream, black, and tan. There are also some patterns you might see like dapple, sable, brindle, or piebald.

Longhaired Dachshund

As suggested by the name, this type of Dachshund has long, silky hair. Most longhaired Dachshunds display some degree of feathering in the fur on their ears and the backs of the legs. These dogs come in the same colors and patterns as the smooth-coated variety but they need a good deal more grooming due to the length and texture of their coats. Some Dachshund owners believe that longhaired Dachshunds have a more docile temperament then the other varieties.

Wirehaired Dachshund

This type of Dachshund coat is not common in the United States but it is popular in Germany and other European nations. The wirehaired Dachshund has a short to medium-length coat of thick, wiry hair that is rough in texture – they also have bushy beards and eyebrows. This type of coat does need daily brushing to prevent mats, but the thickness of the coat helps to protect the dog a little better against cold weather. Wirehaired Dachshunds come in the same colors and patterns, though the wild board coloration (a blend of black, brown, and gray) is popular in the United States, as is the standard black and tan pattern and solid red color.

Chapter Two: Things to Know Before Getting a Dachshund

Now that you have a better understanding of what the Dachshund breed is like you are on your way to making an informed decision whether or not this is the best breed for you. To help you along, in this chapter you will find some practical information about keeping Dachshunds as pets. Here you will learn whether you need a license to keep a Dachshund, whether they get along with other pets, how much it costs to keep a Dachshund as a pet, and some practical pros and cons for the breed.

Do You Need a License?

Before purchasing a Dachshund dog, you should learn about local licensing requirements that may affect you. The licensing requirements for dog owners vary from one country to another so you may need to do a little bit of research on your own to determine whether you need a dog license or not. In the United States, there are no federal requirements for dog licensing – it is determined at the state level. While some states do not, most states require dog owners to license their dogs on an annual basis.

When you apply for a dog license you will have to submit proof that your dog has been given a rabies vaccine. Dog licenses in the United States cost about $25 (£16.25) per year and they can be renewed annually when you renew your dog's rabies vaccine. Even if your state doesn't require you to license your dog it is still a good idea because it will help someone to identify him if he gets lost so they can return him to you.

In the United Kingdom, licensing requirements for dog owners are a little bit different. The U.K. requires that all dog owners license their dogs and the license can be renewed every twelve months. The cost to license your dog in the U.K. is similar to the U.S. but you do not have to have your dog vaccinated against rabies. In fact, rabies does not exist in the U.K. because it was eradicated through careful control measures. If you travel with your dog to or from the U.K., you will have to obtain a special animal moving license and your dog may have to undergo a period of quarantine to make sure he doesn't carry disease into the country.

How Many Dachshunds Should You Keep?

Some dog breeds are very social and they prefer to be kept in a household with other dogs. For Dachshunds, there is no clear answer regarding how they will interact with other dogs and whether they should be kept in multi-dog households. Some Dachshund owners find that their dogs do best in single-dog households but that they can get along with other dogs when they need to. For some Dachshunds, however, having other dogs around may lead to an increase in undesired behavior like barking, especially if the Dachshund feels like he isn't getting enough attention.

If you do plan to keep your Dachshund with other dogs, or if you want to get more than one Dachshund, your best bet is to get all of the dogs at the same time. Many dogs can learn to get along with other dogs when they are raised together from a young age. Just be sure that all of your dogs receive early socialization and training – this will help to minimize problem behaviors in the future.

Do Dachshunds Get Along with Other Pets?

Just as there is no clear answer regarding the Dachshund's ability to get along with other dogs, there is no "yes" or "no" answer to the question regarding Dachshunds and other pets. It is important to keep in mind that Dachshunds were bred from terriers to some degree – this, on top of the fact that they were developed to flush small game, means that they are likely to have a strong prey drive. Some Dachshunds will relentlessly chase cats and other small pets while others show no interest in them at all. Your best bet is to raise your Dachshund with other pets from a young age so he becomes socialized to them.

How Much Does it Cost to Keep a Dachshund?

One of the most important things you need to ask yourself before bringing home a new pet is whether or not you can afford it. Dogs can be very expensive to purchase, especially for purebreds, but you also need to think about monthly costs for food, veterinary care, and other expenses. In this section you will receive an overview of the initial costs and monthly costs for keeping Dachshunds so you can decide whether it is the right pet for you. Be sure you can cover both the initial and monthly costs before you decide to get a Dachshund.

Initial Costs

The initial costs for keeping a Dachshund include those costs that you must cover before you can bring your dog home Some of the initial costs you will need to cover include your dog's crate, food/water bowls, toys and accessories, microchipping, initial vaccinations, spay/neuter surgery and supplies for grooming and nail clipping – it also includes the cost of the dog itself.

You will find an overview of each of these costs as well as an estimate for each cost in the following pages:

Purchase Price – Your biggest initial expense will be the purchase price of your dog. Keep in mind that you will see a wide range of prices when shopping for Dachshund puppies and you shouldn't buy the cheapest puppy you can find – it likely came from a puppy mill or a hobby breeder and it could be carrying inherited diseases. Your best bet is to buy from an AKC-registered breeder or to find a breeder through a national or regional breed club. For a show-quality purebred Dachshund you can expect to pay up to $1,500 (£1,350). For a pet-quality dog, on the other hand, you may be able to find one from an AKC breeder for $500 to $800 (£450 - £720). If you want to adopt an adult Dachshund from a rescue, your costs could be under $200 (£180).

Crate – Because the Dachshund is such a small dog you will not need a very large crate and you probably won't need a different crate for when your dog is a puppy and when he is an adult. The average cost for a small dog crate is about $30 (£19.50) in most cases.

Food/Water Bowls – In addition to providing your Dachshund with a crate to sleep in, you should also make sure he has a set of high-quality food and water bowls. The best materials for these is stainless steel because it is easy to clean and doesn't harbor bacteria – ceramic is another good option. The average cost for a quality set of stainless steel bowls is about $20 (£18).

Toys – Dachshunds are fairly active dogs and they do have a tendency to become destructive when bored. For this reason, you need to have a large assortment of toys on hand to keep your Dachshund busy. To start out, you may want to budget a cost of $50 (£45) for toys just to be sure you have enough to last through the puppy phase.

Microchipping – In the United States and United Kingdom there are no federal or state requirements saying that you have to have your dog microchipped, but it is a very good idea. Your Dachshund could slip out of his collar on a walk or lose his ID tag. If someone finds him without identification, they can take him to a shelter to have his microchip scanned. A microchip is something that is implanted under your dog's skin and it carries a number that is linked to your contact information. The procedure takes just a few minutes to perform and it only costs about $30 (£19.50) in most cases.

Initial Vaccinations – During your dog's first year of life, he will require a number of different vaccinations. If you purchase your puppy from a reputable breeder, he might already have had a few but you'll still need more over the next few months as well as booster shots each year. You should budget about $50 (£32.50) for initial vaccinations just to be prepared.

Spay/Neuter Surgery – If you don't plan to breed your Dachshund you should have him or her neutered or spayed before 6 months of age. The cost for this surgery will vary depending where you go and on the sex of your Dachshund. If you go to a traditional veterinary surgeon, the cost for spay/neuter surgery could be very high but you can save money by going to a veterinary clinic. The average cost for neuter surgery is $50 to $100 (£32.50 - £65) and spay surgery costs about $100 to $200 (£65 - £130).

Supplies/Accessories – In addition to purchasing your Dachshund's crate and food/water bowls, you should also purchase some basic grooming supplies as well as a leash and collar. The cost for these items will vary depending on the quality, but you should budget about $50 (£32.50) for these extra costs.

Initial Costs for Dachshunds		
Cost	**One Dog**	**Two Dogs**
Purchase Price	$200 to $1,500 (£180 - £1,350)	$400 to $3,000 (£360 - £2,700)
Crate	$30 (£19.50)	$60 (£39)
Food/Water Bowl	$20 (£18)	$40 (£36)
Toys	$50 (£45)	$100 (£90)
Microchipping	$30 (£19.50)	$60 (£39)
Vaccinations	$50 (£32.50)	$100 (£65)
Spay/Neuter	$50 to $200 (£32.50 - £130)	$100 to $400 (£65 - £260)
Accessories	$50 (£32.50)	$100 (£90)
Total	$480 to $1,930 (£432 – £1,737)	$960 to $3,760 (£864 – £3,384)

*Costs may vary depending on location
**U.K. prices based on an estimated exchange of $1 = £0.90

Monthly Costs

The monthly costs for keeping a Dachshund as a pet include those costs which recur on a monthly basis. The most important monthly cost for keeping a dog is, of course, food. In addition to food, however, you'll also need to think about things like grooming costs, annual license renewal, toy replacements, and veterinary exams.

You will find an overview of each of these costs as well as an estimate for each cost in the following pages:

Food and Treats – Feeding your Dachshund a healthy diet is very important for his health and wellness. A high-quality diet for dogs is not cheap, so you should be prepared to spend around $35 (£31.50) on a large bag of high-quality dog food which will last you at least a month. You should also include a monthly budget of about $10 (£9) for treats.

Grooming Costs – The cost to groom your Dachshund will vary depending which type of coat he has. Smooth-coated Dachshunds only need occasional brushing and bathing while longhaired and wirehaired Dachshunds need frequent brushing and bathing as well as occasional grooming. To be prepared, you should budget enough for two professional grooming sessions per year. A single session will cost you around $40 (£36), so the cost for two sessions divided over 12 months is about $7 (£6.30) per month.

License Renewal – The cost to license your Dachshund will generally be about $25 (£16.25) and you can renew the license for the same price each year. License renewal cost divided over 12 months is about $2 (£1.30) per month. If you are hestitant ot have your dog licensed, consider the expense of printing "lost dog" posters and the heartache of having to search for your lost pet – you will find that spending a few extra dollars for a dog license is well worth it.

Veterinary Exams – In order to keep your Dachshund healthy you should take him to the veterinarian about every six months after he passes puppyhood. You might have to take him more often for the first 12 months to make sure he gets his vaccines on time. The average cost for a vet visit is about $40 (£26) so, if you have two visits per year, it averages to about $7 (£4.55) per month.

Other Costs – In addition to the monthly costs for your Dachshund's food, grooming, license renewal, and vet visits there are also some other cost you might have to pay occasionally. These costs might include things like replacements for worn-out toys, a larger collar as your puppy grows, cleaning products, and more. You should budget about $15 (£9.75) per month for extra costs.

Monthly Costs for Dachshunds		
Cost	**One Dog**	**Two Dogs**
Food and Treats	$45 (£40.50)	$90 (£81)
Grooming Costs	$7 (£6.30)	$14 to $12.60
License Renewal	$2 (£1.30)	$4 (£3.60)

Veterinary Exams	$7 (£4.55)	$14 (£12.60)
Other Costs	$15 (£9.75)	$30 (£19.50)
Total	$86 to $94 (£78 – £85)	$172 to $188 (£155 - £169)

*Costs may vary depending on location
**U.K. prices based on an estimated exchange of $1 = £0.90

What are the Pros and Cons of Dachshunds?

Before you buy a new pet – no matter what type of pet it is – you need to make sure you understand the ups and the downs. When you are considering buying a Dachshund as a pet it can be tempting to think only about the good things but, if you want to be truly prepared, you need to think about the bad things as well.

You will find a list of pros and cons for the Dachshund dog breed listed below:

Pros for the Dachshund Breed

- Small size makes them a good choice for apartment or condo living; no high exercise needs
- Unique appearance and choice of three different sizes and coat types for the breed

- Smart and trainable for the most part, though some can become stubborn at times
- Short-coated variety is very easy to groom, low shedding
- Very loyal with family, some form very strong attachments with a single person
- Alert and active, generally makes a good watch dog because they bark at strangers

Cons for the Dachshund Breed

- Barking can become a problem, especially with strangers
- Some Dachshunds do not get along well with children, especially young children
- May develop a stubborn streak during training and can sometimes be difficult to housebreak
- Some Dachshunds develop problem behaviors like digging, especially if they are bored
- May develop possessive tendencies with toys, especially if other dogs are present

Chapter Three: Purchasing Your Dachshund

After learning a bit more about the Dachshund breed you should be well on your way to deciding whether or not this is the right breed for you. If you decide that it is, you will have to go through the process of finding a reputable Dachshund breeder and picking out a puppy. Choosing a well-bred, healthy puppy is extremely important if you want your dog to have a long and happy life. In this chapter you will learn about where to find Dachshund puppies, how to choose a reputable breeder, and you will receive tips for picking a healthy puppy from a litter.

Where Can You Buy Dachshunds?

If you are sure that a Dachshund is right for you, you need to start thinking about where you are going to get your new dog. Many people think that the best place to find a dog is at the pet store but, unfortunately, they are greatly mistaken. While the puppies at the pet store might look cute and cuddly, there is no way to know whether they are actually healthy or well-bred. Many pet stores get their puppies from puppy mills and they sell the puppies to unsuspecting dog lovers. Puppy mill puppies are often already sick by the time they make it to the pet store, often traveling across state lines to get there.

A puppy mill is a type of breeding facility that focuses on breeding and profit more than the health and wellbeing of the dogs. Puppy mills usually keep their dogs in squalid conditions, forcing them to bear litter after litter of puppies with little to no rest in between. Many of the breeders used in puppy mills are poorly bred themselves or unhealthy to begin with which just ensures that the puppies will have the same problems. The only time you should bring home a puppy from a pet store is if the store has a partnership with a local shelter and that is where they get their dogs. If the pet store can't tell you which breeder the puppies came from, or if they don't offer you any paperwork or registration for the puppy, it is likely that the puppy came from a puppy mill.

Rather than purchasing a Dachshund puppy from a pet store, your best bet is to find a reputable Dachshund breeder – preferably and AKC-registered breeder in the United States or a Kennel Club-registered breeder in the U.K. If you visit the website for either of these organizations you can find a list of breeders for all of the club-recognized breeds. You can also look for breeders on the website for other breed clubs like the Dachshund Club of America, the National Miniature Dachshund Club, or the UK Dachshund Club. Even if these organizations don't provide a list of breeders you may be able to speak with members through an online forum to find information.

If you don't have your heart set on a Dachshund puppy, consider adopting a rescue from a local shelter. There are many benefits associated with rescuing an adult dog. For one thing, adoption fees are generally under $200 (£180) which is much more affordable than the $500 to $1,500 (£450 to £1,350) fee to buy a puppy from a breeder. Plus, an adult dog will already be housetrained and may have some obedience training as well. As an added bonus, most shelters spay/neuter their dogs before adopting them out so you won't have to pay for the surgery yourself. Another benefit is that an adult dog has already surpassed the puppy stage so his personality is set – with a puppy you can never quite be sure how your puppy will turn out.

If you are thinking about adopting a Dachshund, consider one of these breed-specific rescues:

United States Rescues:

Dachshund Rescue of North America.
<http://www.drna.org/>

All American Dachshund Rescue.
<http://www.allamericandachshundrescue.org/>

Little Paws Rescue. <http://www.littlepawsdr.org/>

Coast to Coast Dachshund Rescue. <http://www.c2cdr.org/>

Furever Dachshund Rescue.
<http://www.fureverdachshundrescue.org/>

Almost Home Dachshund Rescue.
<http://www.almosthomerescue.org/>

You can also try this nationwide list of Dachshund rescues:
<http://dachshundrescuelist.com/>

United Kingdom Rescues:

Dachshund Rescue. <http://www.dachshundrescue.org.uk/>

British Dachshund Rescue.
<http://www.dachshundclub.co.uk/Pages/DachshundRescue
.aspx>

Dachshund Rescue Service.
<http://www.sheffielddirectory.org.uk/kb5/sheffield/director
y/service.page?id=Mebfn3Qu2JI>

Miniature Dachshund Club Rescue.
<http://www.miniaturedachshundclub.co.uk/dachshund_res
cue.htm>

**You can also try this directory of Dachshund rescues from
the UK Kennel Club:**
<http://www.thekennelclub.org.uk/services/public/findaresc
ue/Default.aspx?breed=1012>

How to Choose a Reputable Dachshund Breeder

Finding a Dachshund breeder may be as simple as performing an Internet search, or it might not. If you want to find a reputable breeder of Dachshund puppies, however, you may have to dig a little deeper. When you are ready to start looking for a Dachshund puppy, compile a list of breeders from whatever sources you can and then take the time to go through each option to determine whether the breeder is reputable and responsible or not. You do not want to run the risk of purchasing a puppy from a hobby breeder or from someone who doesn't follow responsible breeding practices. If you aren't careful about where you get your Dachshund puppy you could end up with a puppy that is already sick.

Once you have your list of breeders on hand you can go through them one-by-one to narrow down your options. Go through the following steps to do so:

- Visit the website for each breeder on your list (if they have one) and look for key information about the breeder's history and experience.
  - Check for club registrations and a license, if applicable.

- o If the website doesn't provide any information about the facilities or the breeder you are best just moving on.
- After ruling out some of the breeders, contact the remaining breeders on your list by phone
  - o Ask the breeder questions about his experience with breeding dogs in general and about the Dachshund breed in particular.
  - o Ask for information about the breeding stock including registration numbers and health information.
  - o Expect a reputable breeder to ask you questions about yourself as well – a responsible breeder wants to make sure that his puppies go to good homes.
- Schedule an appointment to visit the facilities for the remaining breeders on your list after you've weeded a few more of them out.
  - o Ask for a tour of the facilities, including the place where the breeding stock is kept as well as the facilities housing the puppies.
  - o If things look unorganized or unclean, do not purchase from the breeder.
  - o Make sure the breeding stock is in good condition and that the puppies are all healthy-looking and active.

- Narrow down your list to a final few options and then interact with the puppies to make your decision.
    - Make sure the breeder provides some kind of health guarantee and ask about any vaccinations the puppies may have already received.
- Put down a deposit, if needed, to reserve a puppy if they aren't ready to come home yet.

By following these steps you can help to ensure that the Dachshund puppy you bring home is well-bred and in good health. This is the best way to give your puppy a chance at a long and healthy life.

Tips for Selecting a Healthy Dachshund Puppy

After you have narrowed down your options for breeders you then need to pick out your puppy. If you are a first-time dog owner, do not let yourself become caught up in the excitement of a new puppy – take the time to make a careful selection. If you rush the process you could end up with a puppy that isn't healthy or one whose personality isn't compatible with your family. Follow the steps below to pick out your Dachshund puppy:

- Ask the breeder to give you a tour of the facilities, especially where the puppies are kept.
  - Make sure the facilities where the puppies are housed is clean and sanitary – if there is evidence of diarrhea, do not purchase one of the puppies because they may already be sick.
- Take a few minutes to observe the litter as a whole, watching how the puppies interact with each other.
  - The puppies should be active and playful, interacting with each other in a healthy way.
  - Avoid puppies that appear to be lethargic and those that have difficulty moving – they could be sick.
- Approach the litter and watch how the puppies react to you when you do.

- o If the puppies appear frightened they may not be properly socialized and you do not want a puppy like that.
- o The puppies may be somewhat cautious, but they should be curious and interested in you.
- Let the puppies approach you and give them time to sniff and explore you before you interact with them.
  - o Pet the puppies and encourage them to play with a toy, taking the opportunity to observe their personalities.
  - o Single out any of the puppies that you think might be a good fit and spend a little time with them.
- Pick up the puppy and hold him to see how he responds to human contact.
  - o The puppy might squirm a little but it shouldn't be frightened of you and it should enjoy being pet.
- Examine the puppy's body for signs of illness and injury
  - o The puppy should have clear, bright eyes with no discharge. The coat should be even and bright white, no patches of hair loss or discoloration.
  - o The ears should be clean and clear with no discharge or inflammation.

- o The puppy's stomach may be round but it shouldn't be distended or swollen.
  - o The puppy should be able to walk and run normally without any mobility problems.
- Narrow down your options and choose the puppy that you think is the best fit.

Once you've chosen your puppy, ask the breeder about the next steps. Do not take the puppy home if it isn't at least 8 weeks old and unless it has been fully weaned and eating solid food.

Puppy-Proofing Your Home

Depending when you visit the breeder, you may still have to wait a few weeks before you can actually bring your Dachshund puppy home. During this time you should take steps to prepare your home, making it a safe place for your puppy. The process of making your home safe for your puppy is called "puppy proofing" and it involves removing or storing away anything and everything that could harm your puppy. It might help for you to crawl around the house on your hands and knees, viewing things from your puppy's perspective in order to identify potential threats.

On the following page you will find a list of some of the things you should do when you are puppy-proofing your home:

- Make sure your trash and recycling containers have a tight-fitting lid or store them in a cabinet.

- Put away all open food containers and keep them out of reach of your puppy.

- Store cleaning products and other hazardous chemicals in a locked cabinet or pantry where your puppy can't get them.

- Make sure electrical cords and blind pulls are wrapped up and placed out of your puppy's reach.

- Pick up any small objects or toys that could be a choking hazard if your puppy chews on them.

- Cover or drain any open bodies of water such as the toilet, and outdoor pond, etc.

- Store any medications and beauty products in the medicine cabinet out of your puppy's reach.

- Check your home for any plants that might be toxic to dogs and remove them or put them out of reach.

- Block off fire places, windows, and doors so your puppy can't get into trouble.

- Close off any stairwells and block the entry to rooms where you do not want your puppy to be.

Chapter Four: Caring for Your Dachshund

After you've done the work of preparing your home for a Dachshund puppy and you've picked one out, all that is left is to give your puppy the best care you can! Caring for a new puppy can be challenging because you not only need to provide for his basic needs, but you also have to train him and socialize him. In this chapter you will find some useful information about the habitat and exercise requirements for the Dachshund breed as well as tips for setting up your puppy's crate in a way that makes him feel at home. In the next chapter you will learn the specifics about caring for your dog's nutritional needs.

Habitat and Exercise Requirements for Dachshunds

The Dachshund is a small-breed dog and some varieties only grow to about 8 pounds. Because these dogs are so small, they make a good choice for apartment and condo living. This is not to say, however, that Dachshunds do not need any exercise – all dogs need a daily walk in order to work off their energy and to remain fit. If you live in an apartment or condo building and do not have a yard where your Dachshund can play for extra exercise, you may need to take him on a slightly longer daily walk.

In addition to providing for your dog's exercise needs, you also need to take certain steps to welcome him into your house. To make your Dachshund comfortable and to ensure that he feels at-home, you will need to provide him with certain things. A crate is one of the most important things you will need when you bring your new Dachshund puppy home. Not only will it be a place for your puppy to sleep, but it will also be a place where you can confine him during the times when you are away from home or when you cannot keep a close eye on him. Your puppy will also need some other basic things like a water bowl, a food bowl, a collar, a leash, toys, and grooming supplies.

When shopping for food and water bowls, safety and sanitation are the top two considerations. Stainless steel is the best material to go with because it is easy to clean and resistant to bacteria. Ceramic is another good option, though it may be a little heavier. Avoid plastic food and water bowls because they can become scratched and the scratches may harbor bacteria. For your dog's collar and leash, choose one that is appropriate to his size. This may mean that you will purchase several collars and leashes while your puppy is still growing. You might also consider a harness – this will be helpful during leash training because it will improve your control over your puppy and it will distribute pressure across his back instead of putting it all on his throat.

Provide your Dachshund puppy with an assortment of different toys and let him figure out which ones he likes. Having a variety of toys around the house is very important because you'll need to use them to redirect your puppy's natural chewing behavior as he learns what he is and is not allowed to chew on. As for grooming supplies, you'll need a wire-pin brush for daily brushing as well as a slicker brush to work through tangles for longhaired and wirehaired Dachshunds. You might also want a metal comb with wide teeth that you can use to work through stubborn mats and some dog-friendly shampoo for baths at home.

Setting Up Your Puppy's Area

Before you bring your Dachshund puppy home, you should set up a particular area in your home for him to call his own. The ideal setup will include your puppy's crate, a comfy dog bed, his food and water bowls, and an assortment of toys. You can arrange all of these items in a small room that is easy to block off or you can use a puppy playpen to give your puppy some free space while still keeping him somewhat confined.

When you bring your puppy home you'll have to work with him a little bit to get him used to the crate. It is very important that you do this because you do not want your puppy to form a negative association with the crate.

You want your puppy to learn that the crate is his own special place, a place where he can go to relax and take a nap if he wants to. If you use the crate as punishment, your puppy will not want to use it.

To get your puppy used to the crate, try tossing a few treats into it and let him go fish them out. Feeding your puppy his meals in the crate with the door open will be helpful as well. You can also incorporate the crate into your playtime, tossing toys into the crate or hiding treats under a blanket in the crate. As your puppy gets used to the crate you can start keeping him in it with the door closed for short periods of time, working your way up to longer periods. Just be sure to let your puppy outside before and after you confine him and never force him to stay in the crate for longer than he is physically capable of holding his bowels and his bladder.

Chapter Five: Meeting Your Dachshund's Nutritional Needs

In addition to making your Dachshund feel at-home in your house, you also need to provide for his nutritional needs. Dachshunds are small dogs so they do not need large quantities of food, but they do require certain nutrients in specific ratios in order to thrive. In this chapter you will receive an overview of the nutritional needs for dogs as well as specific feeding tips for small-breed dogs like the Dachshund. Do not ignore this information! A quality diet is the key to keeping your Dachshund healthy.

The Nutritional Needs of Dogs

Like all mammals, dogs require a balance of protein, carbohydrate and fat in their diets – this is in addition to essential vitamins and minerals. It is important to understand, however, that your dog's nutritional needs are very different from your own. For dogs, protein is the most important nutritional consideration followed by fat and then carbohydrates. In order to keep your dog healthy you need to create a diet that provides the optimal levels of these three macronutrients.

The portion of your dog's diet that comes from protein should be made up of animal sources like meat, poultry, and fish as well as meat meals. Protein is made up of amino acids which are the building blocks that make up your Dachshund's tissues and cells. It also provides some energy for your dog. The most highly concentrated type of energy your Dachshund needs, however, is fat. This nutrient is particularly important for small-breed dogs because they have very fast metabolisms and therefore very high needs for energy.

Consider this – small-breed dogs have higher needs for calories by bodyweight than large dogs. A large-breed dog like a 110-pound Akita, for example, might need a total daily calorie intake of 2,500 calories, but that only amounts to about 23 calories per pound of bodyweight. An 11-pound miniature Dachshund, on the other hand, might only need 450 calories per day but that equates to about 41 calories per pound of its total bodyweight. A significant portion of these calories needs to come from fat in order to meet your dog's nutritional needs.

In addition to protein and fat, your Dachshund also needs carbohydrates to provide dietary fiber and various vitamins and minerals. Dogs do not have a specific need for carbohydrates but they should always come from digestible sources since a dog's digestive tract is not designed to process plant foods as effectively as protein and fat. Your dog also needs plenty of fresh water on a daily basis as well as key vitamins and minerals.

How to Select a High-Quality Dog Food Brand

Shopping for dog food can be difficult for some dog owners simply because there are so many different options to choose from. If you walk into your local pet store you will see multiple aisles filled with bags of dog food from different brands and most brands offer a number of different formulas. So how do you choose a healthy dog food for your Dachshund dog?

The best place to start when shopping for dog food is to read the dog food label. Pet food in the United States is loosely regulated by the American Association of Feed Control Officials (AAFCO) and they evaluate commercial dog food products according to their ability to meet the basic nutritional needs of dogs in various life stages. If the product meets these basic needs, the label will carry some kind of statement from AAFCO like this:

"[Product Name] is formulated to meet the nutritional levels established by the AAFCO Dog Food nutrient profiles for [Life Stage]."

If the dog food product you are looking at contains this statement you can move on to reading the ingredients list. Dog food labels are organized in descending order by volume. This means that the ingredients at the top of the list are used in higher quantities than the ingredients at the end of the list. This being the case, you want to see high-quality sources of animal protein at the beginning of the list. Things like fresh meat, poultry or fish are excellent ingredients but they contain about 80% water. After the product is cooked, the actual volume and protein content of the ingredient will be less. Meat meals (like chicken meal or salmon meal) have already been cooked down so they contain up to 300% more protein by weight than fresh meats.

In addition to high-quality animal proteins, you want to check the ingredients list for digestible carbohydrates and healthy fats. For dogs, digestible carbohydrates include things like brown rice and oatmeal, as long as they have been cooked properly. You can also look for gluten-free and grain-free options like sweet potato and tapioca. It is best to avoid products that are made with corn, wheat, or soy ingredients because they are low in nutritional value and may trigger food allergies in your dog.

In terms of fat, you want to see at least one animal source such as chicken fat or salmon oil. Plant-based fats like flaxseed and canola oil are not necessarily bad, but they are less biologically valuable for your dog. If they are accompanied by an animal source of fat, it is okay. Just make sure that the fats included in the recipe provide a blend of both omega-3 and omega-6 fatty acids. This will help to preserve the quality and condition of your Maltese dog's skin and coat.

In addition to checking the ingredients list for beneficial ingredients you should also know that there are certainly things you do NOT want to see listed. Avoid products made with low-quality fillers like corn gluten meal or rice bran – you should also avoid artificial colors, flavors, and preservatives. Some commonly used artificial preservatives are BHA and BHT. In most cases the label will tell you if natural preservatives are used.

Tips for Feeding Your Dachshund

Once you've chosen a healthy diet for your Dachshund dog you need to know how much and how often to feed him. Because different dog food products have different calorie content you should follow the feeding instructions on the label as a starting point. Most dog food labels provide feeding instructions by weight, so make sure you know how much your dog weighs. It is also important to remember that these are feeding suggestions – you might have to alter the ration for your dog. Dachshunds have a high risk for obesity, so it is very important that you don't overfeed your dog. If your Dachshund starts to gain too much weight with the amount of food you are giving him, decrease his daily ration a little. If he loses weight, increase it a little bit.

In addition to knowing how much to feed your Dachshund you also need to think about how often to feed him. Most dog owners recommend feeding your dog twice a day. Small-breed dogs like the Dachshund have very fast metabolisms, however, so you might want to divide his daily portion over three small meals. As your Dachshund puppy is growing you can feed him freely, allowing him to eat as much as he wants. Once he reaches full size, though, you should start rationing his food.

If you choose a high-quality commercial dog food diet for your Dachshund you can rest easy knowing that his nutritional needs will be met. There are, however, certain nutrients or supplements that can be particularly beneficial for small-breed dogs like the Dachshund. Small-breed dogs tend to have very long lifespans so antioxidants which protect their cells against free radical damage are very important. Antioxidants come from fresh fruits and vegetables, so look for these ingredients in your dog's food. Dogs with spinal and musculoskeletal issues like the Dachshund may also benefit from supplements containing glucosamine and chondroitin to support his bone and joint health over the course of his life.

Dangerous Foods to Avoid

It might be tempting to give in to your dog when he is begging at the table, but certain "people foods" can actually be toxic for your dog. As a general rule, you should never feed your dog anything unless you are 100% sure that it is safe. Below you will find a list of foods that can be toxic to dogs and should therefore be avoided:

- Alcohol
- Apple seeds
- Avocado
- Cherry pits
- Chocolate
- Coffee
- Garlic
- Grapes/raisins
- Hops

- Macadamia nuts
- Mold
- Mushrooms
- Mustard seeds
- Onions/leeks
- Peach pits
- Potato leaves/stems
- Rhubarb leaves
- Tea

- Tomato leaves/stems
- Walnuts

- Xylitol
- Yeast dough

If your Dachshund eats any of these foods, contact the Pet Poison Control hotline right away at (888) 426 – 4435.

Chapter Six: Training Your Dachshund

Once you bring your Dachshund home, the task of training him begins immediately. Puppies are very impressionable while they are young so they learn from each and every experience they have. This can be a good thing if you are intentional about socializing your puppy but it can be a bad thing if you allow your puppy to develop bad habits while he is young. In this chapter you will receive tips for socializing, housebreaking, and training your new Dachshund puppy.

Socializing Your New Dachshund Puppy

The first three months of life is when your Dachshund puppy will be the most impressionable. This is when you need to socialize him because the experiences he has as a puppy will shape the way he interacts with the world as an adult. If you don't properly socialize your Dachshund puppy then he could grow up to be a mal-adjusted adult who fears new experiences – he may also have a greater tendency toward aggression or toward problems with other dogs. Fortunately, socialization is very simple – all you have to do is make sure that your puppy has plenty of new experiences.

<u>Below you will find a list of things you should expose your puppy to for properly socialization</u>:

- Introduce your puppy to friends in the comfort of your own home.

- Invite friends with dogs or puppies to come meet your Maltese (make sure everyone is vaccinated).

- Expose your puppy to people of different sizes, shapes, gender, and skin color.

- Introduce your puppy to children of different ages – just make sure they know how to handle the puppy safely.

- Take your puppy with you in the car when you run errands.

- Walk your puppy in as many places as possible so he is exposed to different surfaces and surroundings.

- Expose your puppy to water from hoses, sprinklers, showers, pools, etc.

- Make sure your puppy experiences loud noises such as fireworks, cars backfiring, loud music, thunder, etc.

- Introduce your puppy to various appliances and tools such as blenders, lawn mowers, vacuums, etc.

- Walk your puppy with different types of harnesses, collars, and leashes.

- Once he is old enough, take your puppy to the dog park to interact with other dogs.

Positive Reinforcement for Obedience Training

Training a dog is not as difficult as many people think – it all has to do with the rewards. Think about this – if you want someone do so something for you, you probably offer them something in return. The same concept is true for dog training – if you reward your dog for performing a particular behavior then he will be more likely to repeat it in the future. This is called positive reinforcement training and it is one of the simplest yet most effective training methods you can use as a dog owner.

The key to success with dog training is two-fold. For one thing, you need to make sure that your dog understands what it is you are asking him. If he doesn't know what a command means it doesn't matter how many times you say it, he won't respond correctly. In order to teach your dog what a command means you should give it and then guide him to perform the behavior. Once he does, immediately give him a treat and praise him – the sooner you reward after identifying the desired behavior, the faster your puppy will learn.

The second key to success in dog training is consistency. While your puppy is learning basic obedience commands you need to use the same commands each and every time and you need to be consistent in rewarding him. If you maintain consistency it should only take a few repetitions for your puppy to learn what you expect of him. You can then move on to another command and alternate between them to reinforce your puppy's understanding. Just be sure to keep your training sessions short – about 15 minutes – so your puppy doesn't get bored.

Keep in mind that many small-breed dogs like the Dachshund develop tendencies toward stubbornness or independence. It is important that you do not punish your dog during training – you can gently correct his behavior, but it is infinitely more effective to reward him for positive behaviors. To work through your Dachshund's stubborn periods, just remain consistent about only rewarding him for good behavior – this will motivate him to follow your commands if he learns that bad behavior doesn't get him what he wants in the end.

Crate Training - Housebreaking Your Puppy

In addition to obedience training, house training is very important for puppies. After all, you don't want to spend your dog's entirely life following after him with a pooper scooper. The key to house training is to use your puppy's crate appropriately. When you are able to watch your puppy, keep him in the same room with you at all times and take him outdoors once every hour or so to give him a chance to do his business. Always lead him to a particular section of the yard and give him a command like

"Go pee" so he learns what is expected of him when you take him to this area.

When you can't watch your puppy and overnight you should confine him to his crate. The crate should be just large enough for your puppy to stand up, sit down, turn around and lie down in. Keeping it this size will ensure that he views the crate as his den and he will be reluctant to soil it. Just make sure that you don't keep your puppy in the crate for longer than he is physically capable of holding his bladder. Always take your puppy out before putting him in the crate and immediately after releasing him.

If you give your puppy ample opportunity to do his business outdoors and you keep him confined to the crate when you can't watch him, housetraining should only take a few weeks. Again, consistency is key here so always reward and praise your puppy for doing his business outside so he learns to do it that way. If your puppy does have an accident, do not punish him because he will not understand – he won't associate the punishment with the crime so he will just learn to fear you instead.

Many people find that small-breed dogs like the Dachshund are difficult to housetrain. If you are having trouble crate training your puppy, do not get frustrated – just keep following the proper procedure and be as consistent with it as possible until your puppy gets the hang of it. It might take a few extra weeks, but your Dachshund will learn eventually.

Chapter Seven: Grooming Your Dachshund

Another task you will need to handle as a dog owner is grooming your dog. Grooming includes brushing and bathing, but it also includes additional tasks like cleaning your dog's teeth and clipping his nails. Each dog responds differently to these kinds of things, so be sure to start early so your Dachshund gets used to being handled – especially when it comes to being groomed by strangers. In this chapter you will receive tips for how and how often to groom your Dachshund as well as valuable information about cleaning his teeth and ears, plus clipping his nails.

Recommended Tools to Have on Hand

If you plan to groom your Dachshund yourself you will need certain tools and supplies. Even if you choose to have your dog professionally groomed, you should still have some supplies available for daily brushing and occasional bathing. Remember, even short-coated Dachshunds should be brushed occasionally, though you will have to groom longhaired and wirehaired dogs more often.

You will find a list of several recommended grooming tools and supplies below:

- Wire-pin brush
- Metal wide-tooth comb
- Slicker brush (or undercoat rake)
- Small, sharp scissors
- Dog-friendly shampoo
- Nail clippers
- Dog-friendly ear cleaning solution
- Dog toothbrush
- Dog-friendly toothpaste

Tips for Bathing and Grooming Dachshunds

Because the longhaired and wirehaired Dachshund has a difficult coat, you may want to have it washed by a professional groomer. Even if you do, you will still need to brush your dog's coat on a daily basis to prevent mats and tangles. Brushing your Dachshund's coat is very easy – just start at the base of the neck and work your way along the dog's back, down his legs, and under his belly. Always brush in the direction of hair growth and move slowly so you don't hurt your dog if you come across a snag.

If you need to bathe your Dachshund, you will want to brush him first. When you are ready for the bath, fill the bathtub with a few inches of warm (not hot) water and place your dog inside. Use a cup to pour water over your dog's back or use a handheld sprayer to wet down his coat. Once your dog's coat is dampened, apply a small amount of dog-friendly shampoo and work it into a lather. After shampooing, rinse your dog's coat thoroughly to get rid of all the soap and then towel him dry. If it is warm you might be able to let his coat air-dry but if it is cold you should finish it off with a blow dryer on the low heat setting.

If you have a longhaired Dachshund, you may also have to worry about trimming his coat. For longhaired Dachshunds that are shown in conformation shows, there may be restrictions regarding how much you can trim the dog's fur. If you are just keeping the dog as a pet, however, you can trim the coat as necessary to make it easier to clean and maintain. Refer to the chapter on Showing Your Dachshund for specific information regarding the show requirements for longhaired Dachshunds.

Other Grooming Tasks

In addition to brushing and bathing your Dachshund, you also need to engage in some other grooming tasks including trimming your dog's nails, cleaning his ears, and brushing his teeth. You will find an overview of each of these grooming tasks below:

Trimming Your Dog's Nails

Your dog's nails grow in the same way that your own nails grow so they need to be trimmed occasionally. Most down owners find that trimming their dog's nails once a week or twice a month is sufficient. Before you trim your

Dachshund's nails for the first time you should have your veterinarian or a professional groomer show you how to do it. A dog's nail contains a quick – the blood vessel that supplies blood to the nail – and if you cut the nail too short you could sever it. A severed quick will cause your dog pain and it will bleed profusely. The best way to avoid cutting your dog's nails too short is to just trim the sharp tip.

Cleaning Your Dog's Ears

The Dachshund has drop ears which means that they hang down on either side of the dog's head. This, combined with the fact that longhaired Dachshund dogs have a lot of hair on and in their ears, increases the dog's risk for ear infections. If the dog's ears get wet it creates an environment that is beneficial for infection-causing bacteria. Keeping your dog's ears clean and dry is the key to preventing infections. If you have to clean your dog's ears, use a dog ear cleaning solution and squeeze a few drops into the ear canal. Then, massage the base of your dog's ears to distribute the solution then wipe it away using a clean cotton ball.

Brushing Your Dog's Teeth

Many dog owners neglect their dog's dental health which is a serious mistake. Small-breed dogs like the Dachshund have a high risk for dental problems because their mouths are so small and their teeth can become overcrowded. You should brush your dog's teeth with a dog-friendly toothbrush and dog toothpaste to preserve his dental health. Feeing your dog dental treats and giving him hard rubber toys can also help to maintain his dental health.

Chapter Eight: Breeding Your Dachshund

If you do not plan to breed your Dachshund, it is recommended by the ASPCA that you have him neutered (or have her spayed) before the age of six months. Not only does this prevent unplanned pregnancies, but it can also reduce your dog's risk for serious diseases and certain types of cancer. If you do choose to breed your dog, be sure to follow responsible breeding practices to ensure the safety of your dogs as well as to prevent the passing of congenital conditions. In this chapter you will receive some information about breeding dogs in general as well as some breed-specific tips for the Dachshund breed.

Basic Dog Breeding Information

Before you decide whether or not to breed your Dachshund, you should take the time to learn the basics about dog breeding in general. If you do not want to breed your dog, the ASPCA recommends having him neutered or her spayed before the age of 6 months. For female dogs, six months is around the time the dog experiences her first heat. Heat is just another name for the estrus cycle in dogs and it generally lasts for about 14 to 21 days. The frequency of heat may vary slightly from one dog to another but it generally occurs twice a year. When your female dog goes into heat, this is when she is capable of becoming pregnant.

When a female dog goes into heat there are a few common signs you can look for. The first sign of heat is swelling of the vulva – this may be accompanied by a bloody discharge. Over the course of the heat cycle the discharge lightens in color and becomes more watery. By the 10th day of the cycle the discharge is light pink – this is when she begins to ovulate and it is when she is most fertile. If you plan to breed your Dachshund, this is when you want to introduce her to the male dog. If the isn't receptive to the male's advances, wait a day or two before trying again.

A dog is technically capable of conceiving at any point during the heat cycle because the male's sperm can survive in her reproductive tract for up to 5 days. If you don't plan to breed your Dachshund you need to keep her locked away while she is in heat. A male dog can smell a female dog in heat from several miles away and an intact male dog will go to great lengths to breed. Never take a female dog in heat to the dog park and be very careful about taking her outside at all. Do not leave her unattended in your backyard because a stray dog could get in and breed with her.

If you want to breed your Dachshund you will need to keep track of her estrus cycle so you know when to breed her. It generally takes a few years for a dog's cycle to become regular and some small-breed dogs go into heat more than twice per year. Keep track of your dog's cycle on a calendar so you know when to breed her. Tracking her cycle and making note of when you introduce her to the male dog will help you predict the due date for the puppies.

Breeding Tips and Raising Puppies

After the male dog fertilizes the egg inside the female's body, the female will go through the gestation period during which the puppies start to develop inside her womb. The gestation period for Dachshund dogs lasts for about 63 to 65 days but you won't be able to actually tell that your dog is pregnant until after the third week. By the 25th day of pregnancy it is safe for a vet to perform an ultrasound and by day 28 he should be able to feel the puppies by palpating the female's abdomen. At the six week mark an x-ray can be performed to check the size of the litter. The average litter size for Dachshunds is 3 to 4 puppies, though many Dachshunds only have 2 and they can have as many as 8 in a single litter. For Miniature Dachshunds, litter sizes are generally 4 puppies.

While the puppies are growing inside your female dog's belly you need to take careful care of her. You don't need to feed your dog any extra until the fourth or fifth week of pregnancy when she really starts to gain weight. Make sure to provide your dog with a healthy diet and keep up with regular vet appointments to make sure the pregnancy is progressing well. Once you reach the fifth week of pregnancy you can increase your dog's daily rations in proportion to her weight gain.

After eight weeks of gestation you should start to get ready for your Dachshund to give birth – in dogs, this is called whelping. You should provide your dog with a clean, safe, and quiet place to give birth such as a large box in a dimly lit room. Line the box with old towels or newspapers for easy cleanup after the birth and make sure your dog has access to the box at all times. As she nears her due date she will start spending more and more time in the box.

When your Dachshund is ready to give birth her internal temperature will decrease slightly. If you want to predict when the puppies will be born you can start taking her internal temperature once a day during the last week of gestation. When the dog's body temperature drops from 100°F to 102°F (37.7°C to 38.8°C to about 98°F (36.6°C), labor is likely to begin very soon. At this point your dog will display obvious signs of discomfort such as pacing, panting, or changing positions. Just let her do her own thing but keep an eye on her in case of complications.

During the early stages of labor, your Dachshund will experience contractions about 10 minutes apart. If she has contractions for more than 2 hours without giving birth, bring her to the vet immediately. Once your Dachshund starts whelping, she will whelp one puppy about every thirty minutes. After every puppy is born, she will clean it with her tongue – this will also help stimulate the puppy to start breathing on its own. After all of the puppies have been born, the mother will expel the afterbirth and the puppies will begin nursing.

It is essential that the puppies start nursing as soon as possible after whelping so that they get the colostrum. The colostrum is the first milk a mother produces and it is loaded with nutrients as well as antibodies that will protect the puppies while their own immune systems continue developing. The puppies will generally start nursing on their own or the mother will encourage them. After the puppies nurse for a little while you should make sure that your mother dog eats something as well.

When they are first born, Dachshund puppies can be very small – the actual size will vary depending on the number of puppies in the litter. Over the next week they will grow fairly quickly and they will continue growing over the next several months until they zone in on their adult size. When Dachshund puppies are born they will have some very fine hair but it isn't enough to keep them warm – your mother Dachshund will help with that. The puppies will be born with their eyes and ears closed but they will start to open around the second or third week following birth.

Your Dachshund puppies will be heavily dependent on their mother for the first few weeks of life until they start becoming more mobile. Around 5 to 6 weeks of age you should start offering your puppies small amounts of solid food soaked in broth or water to start the weaning process. Over the next few weeks the puppies will start to nurse less and eat more solid food. Around 8 weeks of age they should be completely weaned – this is when they are ready to be separated from their mother.

Chapter Nine: Showing Your Dachshund

Dachshunds are among the top 10 most popular dog breeds in the United States according to AKC registration statistics and they are very popular in the show circuit. Because Dachshunds are a pure breed, you will need to make sure your dog adheres to the AKC breed standard before entering him in a show. In this chapter you will learn the details about the Dachshund breed standard and you will also receive some general information about preparing your dog for a show.

Dachshund Breed Standard

The AKC breed standard for the Dachshund breed provides guidelines for both breeding and showing. AKC-registered breeders must select dogs that adhere to the standards of the breed and all Dachshund owners who seek to show their dogs at AKC shows must compare them to the official breed standard as well. <u>Below you will find an overview of the standard for the Dachshund breed</u>:

General Appearance and Temperament

The Dachshund is low to the ground, with a long body and short legs. The muscles are well developed and the skin elastic. The dog is proud and confident with a keen nose and a lively, courageous spirit. He is well-suited for below-ground work – scars from hunting work are not a fault.

Size and Substance

There are two sizes – miniature and standard. Miniatures are a separate classification but in the same class division for 11 pounds and under, weight for standard Dachshunds is between 16 and 32 pounds.

Head and Neck

The head tapers uniformly to the tip of the nose which is dark in color. The eyes are medium-sized and almond shaped, rimmed in black, dark in color. The skull is slightly arched, the muzzle arched, and the bite scissors. The neck is long and muscular without dewlap.

Body and Tail

The trunk is long and well-muscled. The back is a straight line when viewed in profile, the loin slightly arched and the abdomen slightly drawn up. The tail is a continuation of the spine, without twists or kinks.

Legs and Feet

The front legs are strong and cleanly muscled, the chest prominent with well-sprung ribs. The shoulder blades are long and broad, the forearms short but muscled. The hindquarters are strong and cleanly muscled, the paws full and compact with well-arched toes.

Coat and Color

There are three coat types: smooth, wirehaired, and longhaired:

- **Smooth coats** are short and shining, neither too thick nor too thin. The base color is immaterial but certain colors/patterns predominate.
- **Wirehaired Dachshunds** have the whole body covered in tight, thick, rough fur with a soft undercoat and distinctive facial furnishings including beard and eyebrows. Hair is shorter on the ears than the body and almost smooth in texture. All colors and patterns are permissible.
- **Longhaired dogs** have sleek, glistening hair with moderate wave that is longer on the neck and chest as well as the underside of the body, ears, and backs of the legs. The coat should not be too profuse or curly. All colors and patterns are permissible.

Gait

The gait should be smooth and fluid – short and choppy movement is incorrect. Dachshunds are agile with freedom of movement and excellent endurance.

Preparing Your Dachshund for Show

Once you've determined that your Dachshund is a good representation of the official AKC breed standard, then you can think about entering him in a dog show. Dog shows occur all year-round in many different locations so check the AKC or Kennel Club website for shows in your area. Remember, the rules for each show will be different so make sure to do your research so that you and your Dachshund are properly prepared for the show.

Below you will find a list of some general and specific recommendations to follow during show prep:

- Make sure that your Dachshund is properly socialized to be in an environment with many other dogs and people.

- Ensure that your Dachshund is completely housetrained and able to hold his bladder for at least several hours.

- Solidify your dog's grasp of basic obedience – he should listen and follow basic commands.

- Do some research to learn the requirements for specific shows before you choose one – make sure your dog meets all the requirements for registration.

- Make sure that your Dachshund is caught up on his vaccinations (especially Bordetella since he will be around other dogs) and have your vet clear his overall health for show.

- Have your dog groomed about a week before the show and then take the necessary steps to keep his coat clean and in good condition.

In addition to making sure that your Dachshund meets the requirements for the show and is a good representation of the AKC breed standard, you should also pack a bag of supplies that you will need on the day of show. <u>Below you will find a list of helpful things to include in your dog show supply pack:</u>

- Registration information
- Dog crate or exercise pen
- Grooming table and grooming supplies
- Food and treats
- Food and water bowls
- Trash bags

- Medication (if needed)
- Change of clothes
- Food/water for self
- Paper towels or rags
- Toys for the dog

If you want to show your Dachshund but you don't want to jump immediately into an AKC show, you may be able to find some local dog shows in your area. Local shows may be put on by a branch of a national Dachshund breed club and they can be a great place to learn and to connect with other Dachshund owners.

Chapter Ten: Keeping Your Dog Healthy

By now you should have a thorough understanding of the Dachshund breed and what these dogs are like as pets. If you decide that the Dachshund is the right pet for you, you will need to do everything you can to keep your dog in good health. In addition to providing him with a healthy diet, you also need to provide him with routine veterinary care. It will also benefit you to learn which conditions the breed is likely to develop so you can familiarize yourself with the signs and symptoms – this increases your chances of identifying the disease early so your dog can be treated.

Common Health Problems Affecting Dachshunds

The Dachshund is a small-breed dog and this alone means that he has a greater risk for developing spinal problems and other musculoskeletal issues. In this section you will receive an overview of some of the conditions most commonly affecting the Dachshund breed. By educating yourself about the cause, presentation, and treatment for these common conditions you can help to keep your Dachshund in good health for as long as possible.

Some of the common conditions affecting Dachshunds include:

- Allergies
- Diabetes
- Epilepsy
- Eye Problems
- Gastric Torsion
- Intervertebral Disk Disease
- Osteogenesis Imperfecta
- Patellar Luxation
- Patent Ductus Arteriosus
- Periodontal Disease

Allergies

Just like humans, dogs can develop allergic reactions to a number of different things including medications, certain foods, dust, and other environmental pollutants. An allergy develops when the dog's immune system identifies a substance as pathogenic, or dangerous, and it launches an attack. Allergens can be inhaled, ingested, or taken into the body through skin contact. Dogs can develop allergies at any time and some breeds are more prone to allergies than others such as Dachshunds, Terriers, Retrievers, Setters, and brachycephalic breeds like Pugs and Bulldogs.

Common symptoms of allergies in dogs including red or itchy skin, runny eyes, increased scratching, ear infections, sneezing, vomiting, diarrhea, and swollen paws. Some common allergens for dogs include smoke, pollen, mold, dust, dander, feathers, fleas, medications, cleaning products, certain fabrics, and certain foods. Surprisingly, food allergies tend to produce skin-related symptoms like itching and scratching rather than digestive symptoms. Chronic ear infections are also a common sign of food allergies in dogs.

The best treatment for allergies is avoiding contact with the allergen. For some environmental allergens, your vet might prescribe antihistamines or your vet might give your dog an injection to protect him.

Diabetes

Also known as diabetes mellitus, diabetes is a condition that occurs when the dog's body fails to produce enough insulin or its sensitivity to insulin decreases. When your dog eats food, his body starts to break it down into glucose. In response to feeding, the body produces insulin which helps to carry the glucose into the cells where it can be used for energy. If the body doesn't produce enough insulin, or if it cannot use the insulin efficiently, blood glucose (or blood sugar) levels rise and cause a number of different complications.

There are two types of diabetes that dogs can get. Type 1 is inherited and it occurs when the dog's body cannot produce enough insulin. Type 2 is developed and it usually occurs when the dog's response to insulin becomes compromised – this is often correlated with obesity. Symptoms of diabetes in dogs may include changes in appetite, excessive thirst, weight loss, increased urination, lethargy, sweet-smelling breath, vomiting, and chronic skin infections.

Some dogs with diabetes must be given insulin injections to control their blood sugar levels. For others, weight loss and a healthy diet can reverse the effects of the disease. Type 1 diabetes cannot be prevented but a healthy lifestyle may help to prevent the development of Type 2.

Epilepsy

Epilepsy is a seizure disorder that may manifest in several different ways. In most cases, seizures are preceded by a focal onset phase during which the dog may appear dazed or frightened. During the seizure, the dog typically falls to its side and becomes stiff, salivating profusely and paddling with all four limbs. Canine seizures generally last for 30 to 90 seconds and they most commonly occur while the dog is resting or asleep.

There are two types of canine epilepsy – primary and secondary. Primary epilepsy is also called true epilepsy or idiopathic epilepsy – this type of epilepsy involves seizure with an unknown cause. This condition usually presents between 6 months and 5 years of age and it may have a genetic link. Secondary epilepsy is a condition in which the cause of the seizures can be determined. The most common causes for secondary epilepsy include degenerative disease, developmental problems, toxins/poisoning, infections, metabolic disorders, nutritional deficiencies, and trauma.

Veterinarians use information about the age of onset and pattern of the seizures to make a diagnosis. Treatment options for canine epilepsy may involve anticonvulsant medications and monitoring of the dog's health and weight.

Eye Problems

Dachshunds are prone to a number of eye problems, including congenital conditions like cataracts and progressive retinal atrophy. Another common eye problem seen in Dachshunds is glaucoma. Glaucoma is a very common condition in which the fluid inside the dog's eye builds and creates intraocular pressure that is too high. When the pressure inside the eye increases, it can lead to damage of the internal structures within the eye. If this condition is not treated promptly, it can lead to permanent loss of vision or total blindness for the dog.

There are two types of glaucoma – primary and secondary. Primary glaucoma involves physical or physiological traits that increase the dog's risk for glaucoma – this is usually determined by genetics. Secondary glaucoma occurs when the glaucoma is caused by another condition such as a penetrating wound to the eye or other causes for inflammation. Glaucoma can sometimes be difficult to diagnose in the early stages, but common signs include dilated pupil, cloudiness of the eye, and rubbing the eye. Treatment options include topical solutions to reduce pressure, increase drainage, and to provide pain relief.

Progressive retinal atrophy affects the retina of the eye, the part that receives light and converts it into electrical nerve signals that the brain interprets as vision. Dogs with

PRA typically experience arrested retinal development (called retina dysplasia) or early degeneration of the photoreceptors in the eye. Dogs with retinal dysplasia usually develop symptoms within 2 months and are often blind by 1 year.

The signs of PRA vary according to the rate of progression. This disease is not painful and it doesn't affect the outward appearance of the eye. In most cases, dog owners notice a change in the dog's willingness to go down stairs, or to go down a dark hallway – PRA causes night blindness which can progress to total blindness. Unfortunately, there is no treatment or cure for progressive retinal atrophy and no way to slow the progression of the disease. Most dogs with PRA eventually become blind. Fortunately, dogs often adapt well to blindness as long as their environment remains stable.

Cataracts are characterized by an opacity in the lens of the eye which can obstruct the dog's vision. These opacities can be the result of disease, trauma, or old age and they can sometimes be inherited. For the most part, cataracts are not painful but they can sometimes luxate, or slip away from the tissue holding them in place and float around the eye. Sometimes they settle and block fluid drainage which can lead to glaucoma. Cataracts can't be prevented but vision loss can sometimes be corrected with surgery.

Gastric Torsion

Also known as bloat or gastric dilation volvulus, gastric torsion is a condition that most commonly affects large and giant breeds. Because the Dachshund is a very deep-chested breed, however, they are at risk as well. This condition occurs when the animals stomach fills with air and it twists on its axis, cutting off blood flow to and from the stomach. As the condition progresses, the abdomen fills with air and the organs and systems in the dog's body begin to break down from lack of oxygen and blood flow.

Some of the most common symptoms of gastric torsion in dogs include anxiety, depression, and abdominal pain or distended abdomen. Your dog may also start to drool excessively or vomit repeatedly. If the condition isn't corrected, his heart beat will become rapid and he will have trouble breathing. His pulse will weaken and he may fall into a coma or die suddenly.

The exact cause for this condition is unknown but certain things may increase the risk such as consuming large amounts of food or water in a short period of time. Strenuous exercise following a meal or swallowing too much air while eating can lead to gastric torsion as well. Immediate treatment is required to prevent death and surgical options are the most effective. Once treated, most dogs recover within a few weeks.

Intervertebral Disk Disease

Intervertebral disk disease (IVDD) is another musculoskeletal issue common in Corgis. This condition causes a wide variety of different symptoms ranging from mild pain to completely paralysis – it can also mimic the presentation of other musculoskeletal problems which can delay diagnosis. IVDD can occur in any breed, though it is more common in small breeds including the Dachshund.

The symptoms of IVDD are highly variable and may include neck pain or stiffness, back pain or stiffness, abdominal tenderness, arched back, lameness, sensitivity to touch, stilted gait, reluctance to rise, loss of coordination, tremors, collapse, and paralysis. These symptoms most commonly present after strenuous activity of physical trauma. The most common cause of this condition is related to a disorder of cartilage formation called chondrodystrophy and it usually presents in dogs aged 3 to 6 years old.

There are both medical and surgical treatment options available for intervertebral disk disease. Medical treatments may involve corticosteroids or non-steroidal anti-inflammatories aimed to treat pain and control inflammation. Surgical treatments may help to decompress the spinal cord or to inject enzymes to help stabilize the affected disks.

Osteogenesis Imperfecta

Also known as brittle bone disease, osteogenesis imperfecta is the result of an autosomal-recessive genetic defect. This defect affects the development of collagen type 1 in dogs which can cause fragility or brittleness in the bones and teeth. Responsible breeding practices are the best way to prevent this disease. There is a DNA test that breeders can use to see whether a dog is a carrier for the disease so he can decide not to breed that dog – breeding a carrier to a carrier gives the puppies each a 25% chance of developing the disease themselves.

Osteogenesis imperfecta is an inherited condition which means that certain breeds may have a higher risk for it besides the Dachshund. Other breeds at risk for this disease include Poodles, Collies, Golden Retrievers, Bedlington Terriers, and Beagles. Common symptoms of this condition include joint pain, frequent bone and teeth fractures, reduced bone density, and joint hyperlaxity. Blood tests and DNA tests can be used to diagnose the disease, though additional tests may be needed to rule out other causes such as rickets or nutritional deficiencies.

In terms of treatment for osteogenesis imperfecta, there is no definitive therapy and the dog may eventual become lame.

Patellar Luxation

Patellar luxation is a musculoskeletal condition in which the patella (or kneecap) slides out of its normal anatomic position within the groove of the femur (thigh bone). This condition is one of the most common joint abnormalities in dogs and it is particularly common in small and toy breeds like the Dachshund, Pomeranian, Yorkshire Terrier and the Boston Terrier. It is also more common in female dogs than in male dogs.

In the early stages of the condition, many dogs do not display serious symptoms. They might experience some soreness or tenderness after the patella pops back into place but they may still be able to walk normally. The more frequently the dislocation occurs, however, the more wear and tear on the bone and joint the dog will suffer. This leads to osteoarthritis and pain, potentially even lameness in the joint. The dog generally doesn't experience pain while the kneecap is dislocated, but he will when it pops back into its rightful place.

The cause of patellar luxation is usually the result of a genetic malformation or some kind of trauma. Unfortunately, medical treatments are rarely effective and surgery is usually required to achieve long-term relief. After surgery the dog will need to limit its mobility and regular vet check-ups are recommended.

Patent Ductus Arteriosus

Often shortened to PDA, patent ductus arteriosis is a congenital heart defect known to affect the Dachshund and other breeds. This defect is caused by incomplete changes in the way the heart circulates blood when the puppy is born. The ductus arteriosis is the name for one of the main blood vessels in the heart that helps to keep blood from flowing into the lungs while the fetus is still in the womb (the lungs don't need the blood because the fetus isn't breathing fresh air yet). When the puppy is born, the vessel is supposed to close off naturally within a few hours, allowing the blood to flow normally to the lungs, but in cases of patent ductus arteriosis it remains open.

This condition can be very serious and life-threatening for puppies. Common symptoms include shortness of breath, coughing, weakness, and reduced tolerance for exercise. As the disease progresses, the puppy may develop signs of heart failure. If surgery isn't performed to close the vessel, the puppy will eventually die from heart failure. There are several different surgical methods for correcting the issue and, in most cases, the dog recovers completely. A repeat ECG is recommended after 3 months to check and long-term follow-up appointments may be recommended as well.

Periodontal Disease

Also known as gum disease, periodontal disease is incredibly common in dogs - it is particularly common in small-breed dogs like the Dachshund because their teeth tend to get crowded in their small skulls. Most dogs develop some level of gum disease by the time they are three years old. In most cases, dogs with periodontal disease do not show any signs in the early stages. As the disease progresses, however, the dog might experience pain, eroded gums, and even tooth or bone loss. At this point, the only treatment option is to remove the affected teeth.

After your dog eats, saliva, food particles and bacteria accumulate on the surface of the teeth in a film called plaque. Over time, the plaque hardens into a calculus known as tartar which can then start to spread under the gum line and into the root of the tooth and the bone beneath. The bacteria can also make its way into your dog's blood stream, causing serious infections.

As periodontal disease progresses you may notice signs like bleeding or red gums, loose teeth, difficulty chewing, bad breath, or ropey saliva. It is very important that your dog gets regular dental checkups as part of his veterinary exams – you should also have your dog's teeth cleaned once a year. To maintain your dog's dental health, brush his teeth daily.

Preventing Illness with Vaccinations

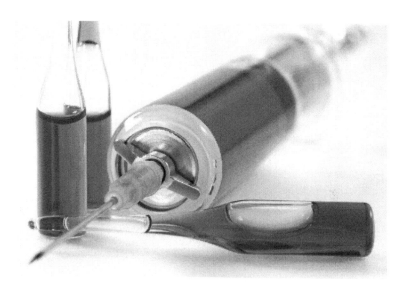

Providing your Dachshund with a healthy diet and regular veterinary care are two of the most important ways to maintain his health – vaccinations are also important. Having your dog vaccinated will help to protect him from certain deadly diseases like rabies, distemper, and parvovirus. The vaccinations your Dachshund needs may vary depending where you live since certain regions have a higher risk for certain diseases. Your vet will know which vaccinations your dog needs and when he needs them, but the vaccination schedule below will help you to keep track of when your Dachshund needs to see the vet.

To give you an idea what kind of vaccinations your puppy will need, consult the vaccination schedule below:

Vaccination Schedule for Dogs**			
Vaccine	**Doses**	**Age**	**Booster**
Rabies	1	12 weeks	annual
Distemper	3	6-16 weeks	3 years
Parvovirus	3	6-16 weeks	3 years
Adenovirus	3	6-16 weeks	3 years
Parainfluenza	3	6 weeks, 12-14 weeks	3 years
Bordetella	1	6 weeks	annual
Lyme Disease	2	9, 13-14 weeks	annual
Leptospirosis	2	12 and 16 weeks	annual
Canine Influenza	2	6-8, 8-12 weeks	annual

** Keep in mind that vaccine requirements may vary from one region to another. Only your vet will be able to tell you which vaccines are most important for the region where you live.

Dachshund Care Sheet

In reading this book you have received a wealth of information about the Dachshund breed including details of its care and keeping. When you bring your own Dachshund home, you will be glad to have this book on hand as a resource while you learn the ins and outs of dog ownership. You may find that you occasionally need to reference a certain bit of information but you may not want to flip through the entire book to find it. In this section you will find a care sheet which includes all of the valuable tidbits you need regarding the care and keeping of Dachshunds.

1.) Basic Dachshund Information

Pedigree: origins may be traced to ancient Egypt; modern breed developed from European hounds and terriers

AKC Group: Hound Group

Breed Size: small

Height: 8 to 9 inches (Standard); 4 to 6 inches (Miniature)

Weight: 16 to 32 pounds (Standard); up to 11 pounds (Miniature); 8 to 11 pounds (Kaninchen)

Coat Length: smooth, longhaired or wirehaired

Coat Texture: soft and short; long and silky with feathering on the ears and legs; medium-length, harsh and wiry

Color: many colors and patterns; base color of red or cream is common, often with tan color points; no standard color

Eyes and Nose: ranges from amber to dark brown or green; AKC prefers darker colors

Ears: large, floppy drop ears

Tail: medium-length, thin and tapered

Temperament: playful, smart, active, clever, sometimes stubborn, prone to barking

Strangers: may bark at strangers, good watch dog

Children: may not be a good choice for young children

Other Dogs: generally good with other dogs if properly trained and socialized; may bark at other dogs

Training: intelligent and trainable but can develop a stubborn streak; may be tricky to housebreak

Exercise Needs: playful and active; need a moderate amount of exercise; prone to problem behaviors with boredom

Health Conditions: back problems, disc injuries, gastric torsion, diabetes, epilepsy, eye problems, skin conditions, obesity, patellar luxation

Lifespan: average 12 to 15 years

2.) Habitat Requirements

Recommended Accessories: crate, dog bed, food/water dishes, toys, collar, leash, harness, grooming supplies

Collar and Harness: sized by weight

Grooming Supplies: wire pin brush, slicker brush, metal wide-tooth comb

Grooming Frequency: brush daily; professional grooming twice a year for longhaired Dachshunds

Energy Level: active but no high exercise needs

Exercise Requirements: 30 minute walk daily

Crate: highly recommended

Crate Size: just large enough for dog to lie down and turn around comfortably

Crate Extras: lined with blanket or plush pet bed

Food/Water: stainless steel or ceramic bowls, clean daily

Toys: start with an assortment, see what the dog likes; include some mentally stimulating toys

Exercise Ideas: play games to give your dog extra exercise during the day; train your dog for various dog sports

3.) Nutritional Needs

Nutritional Needs: water, protein, carbohydrate, fats, vitamins, minerals

Calorie Needs: varies by age, weight, and activity level

Amount to Feed (puppy): feed freely but consult recommendations on the package

Amount to Feed (adult): consult recommendations on the package; calculated by weight

Feeding Frequency: two to three meals daily

Important Ingredients: fresh animal protein (chicken, beef, lamb, turkey, eggs), digestible carbohydrates (rice, oats, barley), animal fats

Important Minerals: calcium, phosphorus, potassium, magnesium, iron, copper and manganese

Important Vitamins: Vitamin A, Vitamin A, Vitamin B-12, Vitamin D, Vitamin C

Look For: AAFCO statement of nutritional adequacy; protein at top of ingredients list; no artificial flavors, dyes, preservatives

4.) Breeding Information

Age of First Heat: around 6 months (or earlier)

Heat (Estrus) Cycle: 14 to 21 days

Frequency: twice a year, every 6 to 7 months

Greatest Fertility: 11 to 15 days into the cycle

Gestation Period: average 63 to 65 days

Pregnancy Detection: possible after 21 days, best to wait 28 days before exam

Feeding Pregnant Dogs: maintain normal diet until week 5 or 6 then slightly increase rations

Signs of Labor: body temperature drops below normal 100° to 102°F (37.7° to 38.8°C), may be as low as 98°F (36.6°C); dog begins nesting in a dark, quiet place

Contractions: period of 10 minutes in waves of 3 to 5 followed by a period of rest

Whelping: puppies are born in 1/2 hour increments following 10 to 30 minutes of forceful straining

Puppies: born with eyes and ears closed; eyes open at 3 weeks, teeth develop at 10 weeks

Litter Size: average 3 to 4 puppies (standard); miniature Dachshunds often have 4 puppies

Size at Birth: varies greatly depending on the size of the litter (larger litters generally have smaller puppies)

Weaning: start offering puppy food soaked in water at 6 weeks; fully weaned by 8 weeks

Socialization: start as early as possible to prevent puppies from being nervous as an adult

Index

C

D

E

F

G

Q

R

S

T

U

V

W

References

"A Few Dachshund Breeding Guidelines." Dachshund
   World. <http://www.dachworld.com/breedingrules.htm>

"AAFCO Dog Food Nutrient Profiles." DogFoodAdvisor.
   <http://www.dogfoodadvisor.com/frequently-asked-
   questions/aafco-nutrient-profiles/>

"Annual Dog Care Costs." PetFinder.
   <https://www.petfinder.com/pet-adoption/dog-
   adoption/annual-dog-care-costs/>

"Buying and Owning a Dachshund." Dachshund Breed
   Council. <https://dachshundbreedcouncil.files.wordpress.
   com/2011/12/buy_and_own_e-book.pdf>

"Canine Dental Disease." Banfield Pet Hospital.
   <http://www.banfield.com/pet-health-
   resources/preventive-care/dental/canine-dental-disease>

"Choosing a Healthy Puppy." WebMD.
   <http://pets.webmd.com/dogs/guide/choosing-healthy-

"Dachshund." DogTime.com. <http://dogtime.com/dog-
   breeds/dachshund

"Dachshund." VetStreet.
   <http://www.vetstreet.com/dogs/dachshund#history>

"Dachshund Dogs." Dogster. <http://www.dogster.com/dog-
   breeds/Dachshund>

"Dachshund Temperament." Your Purebred Puppy. <http://www.yourpurebredpuppy.com/reviews/dachshunds.html>

"Dachshund Temperament and Personality." PetWave.com. <http://www.petwave.com/Dogs/Breeds/Dachshund/Personality.aspx>

"How to Find a Responsible Breeder." HumaneSociety.org. <http://www.humanesociety.org/issues/puppy_mills/tips/finding_responsible_dog_breeder.html?referrer=https://www.google.com/>

"How Much do Dachshund Puppies Cost?" HowMuchIsIt.org. <http://www.howmuchisit.org/dachshund-puppies-cost/>

"Most Popular Dog Breeds in America." AKC.org. <http://www.akc.org/news/the-most-popular-dog-breeds-in-america/>

"My Bowl: What Goes into a Balanced Diet for Your Dog?" PetMD. <http://www.petmd.com/dog/slideshows/nutrition-center/my-bowl-what-goes-into-a-balanced-diet-for-your-dog>

"Nutrients Your Dog Needs." ASPCA.org. <https://www.aspca.org/pet-care/dog-care/nutrients-your-dog-needs>

"Nutrition: General Feeding Guidelines for Dogs." VCA Animal Hospitals. <http://www.vcahospitals.com/

main/pet-health-information/article/animal-health/nutrition-general-feeding-guidelines-for-dogs/6491>

"Official Standard of the Dachshund." American Kennel Club. <http://images.akc.org/pdf/breeds/standards/Dachshund.pdf?_ga=1.217191126.1751144016.1454425532>

"Pet Care Costs." ASPCA.org. <https://www.aspca.org/adopt/pet-care-costs>

"Pregnancy and Whelping." Dachshund World. <http://www.dachworld.com/pregnancywhelping.htm>

"Puppy Proofing Your Home." Hill's Pet. <http://www.hillspet.com/dog-care/puppy-proofing-your-home.html>

"Puppy Proofing Your Home." PetEducation.com. <http://www.peteducation.com/article.cfm?c=2+2106&aid=3283>

Vitamins and Minerals Your Dog Needs." Kim Boatman. The Dog Daily. <http://www.thedogdaily.com/dish/diet/dogs_vitamins/index.html#.VHOtMPnF_IA>

"When Your Dog Gets Sick." Dachshund World. <http://www.dachworld.com/sickdogs.htm>

Photo Credits

**All photos purchased from BigStockPhoto.net unless otherwise noted

Page 17 (Smooth Coated Dachshund) by Igor Bredikhin via Wikimedia Commons, <https://en.wikipedia.org/wiki/ File:Short-haired-Dachshund.jpg>

Page 18 (Longhaired Dachshund) by Lilly M via Wikimedia Commons, <https://en.wikipedia.org/wiki/Dachshund#/ media/File:Jamnik_d%C5%82ugow%C5%82osy_standardow y_LM_671.jpg>

Page 19 (Wirehaired Dachshund) by Janne Seppanen via Wikimedia Commons, <https://en.wikipedia.org/wiki/ Dachshund#/media/File:Jamnik_d%C5%82ugow%C5%82osy _standardowy_LM_671.jpg>

Page 44 (Dachshund Puppy) by Lachlan Hardy via Wikimedia Commons, <https://commons.wikimedia.org/ wiki/File:Smooth_Miniature_Dachshund_puppy.jpg>

Page 81 (Dachshund Puppies) by Alex Khimich via Wikimedia Commons, <https://commons.wikimedia.org/wiki/File:Dachshund-puppies.jpg>

Feeding Baby
Cynthia Cherry
978-1941070000

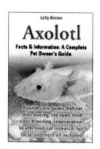

Axolotl
Lolly Brown
978-0989658430

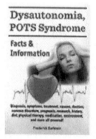

Dysautonomia, POTS
Syndrome
Frederick Earlstein
978-0989658485

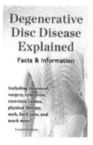

Degenerative Disc
Disease Explained
Frederick Earlstein
978-0989658485

Sinusitis, Hay Fever,
Allergic Rhinitis Explained
Frederick Earlstein
978-1941070024

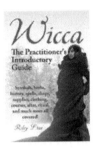

Wicca
Riley Star
978-1941070130

Zombie Apocalypse
Rex Cutty
978-1941070154

Capybara
Lolly Brown
978-1941070062

Eels As Pets
Lolly Brown
978-1941070167

Scabies and Lice Explained
Frederick Earlstein
978-1941070017

Saltwater Fish As Pets
Lolly Brown
978-0989658461

Torticollis Explained
Frederick Earlstein
978-1941070055

Kennel Cough
Lolly Brown
978-0989658409

Physiotherapist, Physical
Therapist
Christopher Wright
978-0989658492

Rats, Mice, and Dormice
As Pets
Lolly Brown
978-1941070079

Wallaby and Wallaroo Care
Lolly Brown
978-1941070031

Bodybuilding Supplements
Explained
Jon Shelton
978-1941070239

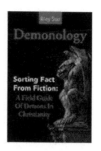

Demonology
Riley Star
978-19401070314

Pigeon Racing
Lolly Brown
978-1941070307

Dwarf Hamster
Lolly Brown
978-1941070390

Cryptozoology
Rex Cutty
978-1941070406

Eye Strain
Frederick Earlstein
978-1941070369

Inez The Miniature Elephant
Asher Ray
978-1941070353

Vampire Apocalypse
Rex Cutty
978-1941070321

Printed in Poland
by Amazon Fulfillment
Poland Sp. z o.o., Wrocław